William Nicholas Hailmann

Application of the Principles of Psychology to the Work of Teaching

Teaching

William Nicholas Hailmann

Application of the Principles of Psychology to the Work of Teaching

ISBN/EAN: 9783337165734

Printed in Europe, USA, Canada, Australia, Japan

Cover: Foto ©Thomas Meinert / pixelio.de

More available books at **www.hansebooks.com**

APPLICATION

OF THE

PRINCIPLES OF PSYCHOLOGY

TO THE

WORK OF TEACHING.

BY

W. N. HAILMANN, A. M.,

AUTHOR OF "KINDERGARTEN CULTURE," "HISTORY OF PEDAGOGY," ETC.

Published by order of the Board of Directors,

BOSTON,
WILLARD SMALL,
1884.

\

Press of W. F. Brown & Co., 218 Franklin St.

CONTENTS.

PREFACE.

At no previous time in the history of education in this country have teachers and School Superintendents manifested a more earnest desire to understand the philosophy of their work. Everything written upon the subject is read with interest. The American Institute of Instruction, through the Trustees of the Bicknell Fund, awarded the entire income of that Fund for the year 1883, to the best essay upon the Application of the Principles of Psychology to the work of Teaching. The committee of award consisted of J. W. Dickinson, Mrs. E. N. L. Walton, and George H. Martin. Within the limit of time allowed for presenting the essays, thirty were received. Among these were others of considerable merit; but to the essay by Prof. Hailmann, the committee made the award with entire unanimity.

By the conditions of the award, the essay receiving the prize becomes the exclusive property of the Institute. Electrotype plates have been made, and an edition of this essay is published, to facilitate a study which must be more and more pursued, as progress is made in the art of teaching. The abstract read at the Annual Meeting of the Institute, was received with much favor, and it is believed the publication at the present time will meet a general demand.

Boston, May, 1884.

The Application of the Principles of Psychology to the Work of Teaching.

EDUCATION comprises all intentional and systematic influences upon the development of the human being, particularly of the young human being or child.

This definition at once separates educational factors into two groups, — the conscious and the unconscious factors. Among the former, the principal ones are the parents or their substitutes, the teacher, and the child himself. Among the unconscious factors, the leading ones are the nature of the child (i. e., the inner growth of its powers), surroundings, and society, as long as it has no direct interest in the child.

We are here concerned only with the teacher. Yet the principles involved apply with equal force to all educational work. Hence we take no cognizance of the narrower aim in the statement of these principles.

The unconscious factors can exert an educational influence, only if one or several of the conscious factors aid them. The richest surroundings produce no effect upon the child, if he takes no interest in them; hence it is one of the chief tasks of the educator to arouse and direct this interest, and to render it consciously self-educative. The inner growth of the child's powers, his nature, may go astray or stop progress wholly, if conscious educators do not

guide and foster it, or if the child himself, after reaching a
certain maturity, does not consciously keep it in the right
direction. Natural development, surroundings, and all
other unconscious factors alone, can no more educate than
the hammer alone can forge, or the unguided stream drive
the mill wheel. They need, in order to become efficient,
the directing hand of the master.

This view of education imposes upon educators the
necessity of devising a fixed plan for their work in aims
and means. The whole work should tend in every part
towards distinct ideals; and the path followed should be
carefully adapted to these ideals, and to the nature and
destiny of the child.

The choice of the educational ideal is of primary importance, since upon it depends the value of the education to
the child and to society. Of course, the educators have no
right to choose ideals that deprive the human being of his
liberty, render him hostile to society, or give him only a
transient and relative value. The ideals they have a right
to choose, should give the human being freedom in the
exercise of all his powers, with constant reference to the
welfare of society and the advancement of the race, and
should impart to him a lasting and absolute value. They
should lead his taste to the Beautiful, his insight to Truth,
his conduct to the Good.

Only wisdom whose essence is the striving for truth, and
virtue whose essence is the striving for goodness, can give
man a lasting and absolute value, — a value which no
vicissitudes of life can diminish, which will enable him to
scatter love and to gather peace. All that fails to lead to
these, all that hinders development towards these, all that
refuses to heed the requirements of the Beautiful, the
True, and the Good, these highest criteria of feeling,

thought and conduct, is false education, and cannot be considered here.

In his nature, the human being appears as a growing organism. He develops from within outward, according to certain organic laws which apply with equal force to all the phases of his being. He appears as a distinct unity in conscious opposition to all else; a self-knowing within, placed over against an all-embracing without; a growing microcosm, placed within a sustaining macrocosm; a node, where infinity outward and infinity inward enter into consciousness.

For purposes of study, it has been customary to subdivide his nature in various ways; but it should be remembered that these subdivisions exist only in and for science, not in man. Thus the phases of his being, which lie between the within and the without, and through which his self is impressed by the external or impresses the latter, constitute his *physical* nature. His *psychical* nature enables him to comprehend the finite actualities in time and space; and his *spiritual* nature reveals to him the infinite potentialities, which are the essence of all being. Thus, too, the successive conditions of knowing, feeling, and willing are but the three successive stages of one and the same mental process of complete cerebration, in which the conscious personality sees, becomes interested, and reacts.

The consideration of man's nature reveals to us also his destiny. This appears to us as the conscious acknowledgment, in all the phases of life, of the unity which is in him and which, at the same time, makes him one with all, — a self-conscious utterance of the Infinite. It appears as the establishment in consciousness of full accord, between the inner and the outer; between the microcosm and the macrocosm; between seeing, feeling, and doing; between experience and practice.

Practically, this implies mastership, or control. Objectively, it means control of surroundings, of the world; subjectively, it means obedience to the laws of being, or control of self. The conditions of control are knowledge of the object to be mastered, knowledge of one's own powers, and skill in applying or wielding the latter, in establishing the needed harmony between self and the object in question. Knowledge comes from observation and experience, skill comes from practice. · It may, therefore, be said that, proximately, the destiny of man is to establish harmony between observation and experience on the one hand, and practice on the other.

When we apply this to individual human beings it seems quite trivial; but not so when applied to man in his relations to mankind. Here we find him profiting by the garnered knowledge of past ages, and adding to this the increase gained by him; here we see him appropriating the observation and experience of his generation, and scattering broadcast among his own contemporaries the yield of his own life; here he submits in his practice to the judgment of men long dead, or lays down rules for the practice of his children's children; here he co-ordinates his will to that of thousands, for the sake of a mastership which needs the combined energy of many, or thousands become willing tools of his determination in the service of a common advantage; here we find man in relationships that free him from the fetters of time and space, and open to him the realms of the Infinite.

Psychology is concerned with the study of the phenomena 'of consciousness. The growth and development of consciousness, the natural history of ideas, emotions, and volitions, of knowing, feeling, and willing, — constitute its province. From the time when an influence from without has produced a change within, directly — though ever so remotely — connected with the subsequent arousal of consciousness, this change becomes an object of interest to psychology, and remains so, as long as it continues to exert any influence through consciousness upon the conduct.

Strictly speaking, psychology has no interest in those influences from without as such, nor with the actions themselves which in their aggregate constitute conduct, nor indeed, with the physical concomitants of cerebration in the body of man. Nevertheless the entire nervous apparatus, and particularly that of the senses, is so intimately connected with the origin and evolution of the facts of consciousness; and the reflex influence of action upon ideas, feelings, and the will, is so great that their consideration is of the utmost importance in applying psychological principles to education.

In its general features, the course of psychological development is simple enough. Through the agency of the senses, outer influences cause disturbances in inner equilibrium, or *sense-impressions.* These in due time become sufficiently numerous or intense to arouse *attention*, and consciousness is born. So far the process has been mainly, if not exclusively, inward; but very soon a reaction sets in by which the attention is directed outward, towards the outer concomitants of the inner disturbances. These outer concomitants are found, the mind perceives their unity with corresponding inner forms of consciousness: it has gained *perceptions.*

The inner disturbances of equilibrium, underlying these formations, are more or less permanent in the *memory.*

They may be brought back to consciousness in various ways, involuntarily by closely related disturbances from without or within, or voluntarily for purposes of thought or feeling, when the mind *remembers* or *recollects*, *fancies* or *imagines*.

The frequent re-arousing of perceptions, containing similar and dissimilar features, gives to the similar or common features in due time a certain prominence over other features ; these assume a *quasi*-independent existence, approaching objectivity, in the outer regions of consciousness. To these *conceptions* the mind constantly refers its perceptions, and they become the inner concomitants of language.

Subsequently this growing consciousness learns to dif-. ferentiate itself from the external more and more clearly, to recognize itself as *subject*, distinct from all else, as *object*. Its concepts grow more and more distinct, as well as more comprehensive ; it begins to understand relations in the actual more and more clearly : it has grown into an *intellect*.

At last the intellect learns to look upon itself objectively, as it were ; learns to see essential relations between the inner and the outer, as well as among the inner and outer respectively ; discovers the intimate relationship existing between the inner microcosm whose soul is time, and the outer macrocosm whose soul is space : it obtains an *insight* into relations that partake of the Infinite, it has acquired the power of *reason*, and has risen to the dignity of *spirit*.

Thus the mind rises successively from the sensual, through the intellectual, to the spiritual phase on the side of thought.

A similar process accompanies this on the side of feeling.

In simple *sensation*, the common root of insight and emotion, the sense impression is still so closely blended with the corresponding feeling that it is quite difficult to distinguish the two. Hence the same term sensation, designates almost indiscriminately either or both.

As soon, however, as the mind has discovered the unity between the inner and the outer in perception, it has also learned to apprehend beneath the knowledge, and deeper within itself, as even more fully its own, the attendant feeling of pleasure or pain. This apprehension lives in consciousness as *desire* to hold or relinquish the corresponding form of thought.

Consciousness becomes more and more involved in this desire, until the mind learns to connect it more and more clearly with certain external conditions and their relation to inner welfare. It then begins to take a lively and more or less permanent *interest* in the study of these conditions, an interest which is the mainspring of intellectual activity.

When, at last, the intellect has become interested in itself as an object of thought, the feelings aroused by the discovery of self in its inward and outward relations to the Infinite, the consonances and dissonances of being thrill the mind in its innermost depths, in *emotions* that fill it to the momentary exclusion of all else, and infuse it with an intense yearning for fixing the harmonies or resolving the disharmonies in suitable action.

Of these yearnings there is born, in due time, a persistent energy of action, which directs man towards certain objects or purposes. It takes thought into its service, as counselor or guide; assumes control of man; and, as *will*, is crowned the sovereign on whose wisdom depends the value of life, inwardly and outwardly.

These are some of the landmarks set up by science in

her efforts to grasp mental growth. It should be remembered, however, and more particularly when we would
apply these matters in education, that the transition from
one form to another is so gradual and so continuous that it
is impossible to find any form stopping, as it were, at the
landmarks of science. The forms are always on the move,
approaching the point of observation or passing beyond it.

Besides, the infinite mobility of mental being involves
such a complexity of co-existent mental forms, that the
mental condition at any given moment is the resultant of
an infinite variety of mental activities in all possible stages
of development.

Similar difficulties meet us when we approach the subject on the side of *action*, of the outward reactions or
utterances of mental states in the various forms of moving,
voicing, and doing. As soon as sense-impressions begin to
be formed, the mind reacts in a variety of such utterances,
more or less to the point. Similarly, perceptions and
desires, conceptions and interests, insight and emotion
react outwardly in a manner so direct and to the point, that
it is difficult to distinguish these actions, with reference to
their sources, not only from each other, but even from
those of the will.

In fact, all these actions and utterances are as complex
in their sources as the mind is in its conditions of consciousness. Hence, practically, the first utterances of new-
born consciousness have somewhat of the will in them ;
while, on the other hand, the actions of the maturest will
are more or less influenced by lower forms of thought and
feeling.

However, some scheme like the one indicated above is
indispensable for systematic educational work. For more
convenient survey, therefore, the chief features of that

scheme are presented below in condensed form, roughly tabulated.

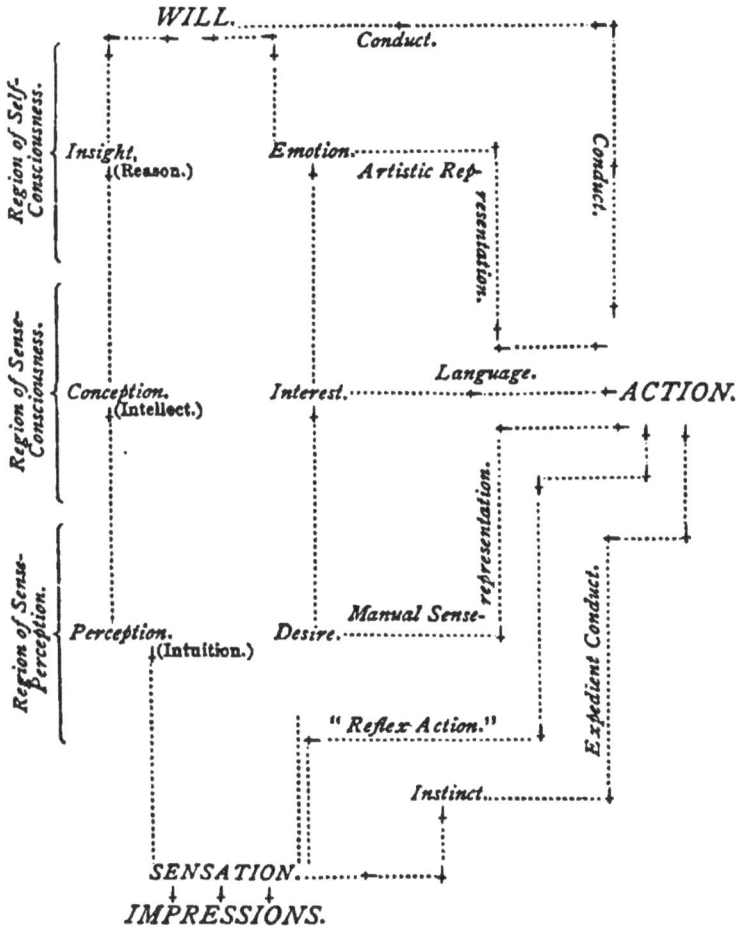

The only additional explanation that is needed concerns the place of the *instinct*. This has been purposely placed at one side of the main table, as a form of reaction in the feelings, attending sensation, but playing a vanishingly subordinate part in the development of the human will, which is the chief concern of education. Instinct appears as a vigorous offshoot of inner reaction with much native energy, sufficient in the lower forms of life to rise to a wonderfully high degree of perfection in securing expedience of action.

In the application of these principles to education, it is further necessary to take into account the reflex influence which in any given psychological process runs back from action to its source. Action, in satisfying a desire, in gratifying an interest, in expressing an emotion, by a reflex influence strengthens, purifies, idealizes these forms of feeling, and through them their corresponding forms in thought. Hence, action is a most powerful instrument in the hands of the educator for quickening all forms of thought-growth, from perception to insight.

Through action, the internal becomes external ; the inner assumes an outer existence in the terms of the outer. Thus an opportunity is afforded for testing the correctness of the inner conceptions, with reference to their outer concomitants, by *quasi*-direct comparison. The contrasts between the original outer concomitant and the outer reproduction of the conception appear as inaccuracies, deficiencies, exaggerations, and other faults that call for correction. Thus action pushes conception steadily and surely nearer to objective truth.

It is for a similar reason that language plays so important a part in mental growth. It is true, words are but symbols of the inner thought-forms, incapable of the objective reality of plastic or graphic ·representation. They merely arouse in the mind of the hearer the corresponding thought-form in terms of his own subjective thought. Yet they are capable of expressing relations of being with almost specific precision and clearness. Hence, language is the chief instrument of the mind in its analyses and syntheses of observation or invention, of fancy or imagination.

If *plastic* and *graphic* sense-representations are of the utmost value in establishing a substratum of reliable perceptions, *language* is indispensable in the operations of the intellect, while the needs of the creative spirit are supplied by *art*. In their essence, however, all sense-representation, language, and art are but variations of action, and owe their educational value to the reflex influence of action upon mental development.

In the case of the will, action appears a *conduct*, which as *practice*, exerts a powerful reflex influence in fixing the will into *habit*, and establishing the *character*.

The primary conditions under which psychological development takes place are, then, the following: First, an active external, capable of making impressions; second, an active internal, capable of actively receiving these impressions, of spontaneously placing itself in consciousness, opposite all else, and of controlling the external for inner needs. And, primarily, the business of education is to adjust surroundings with reference to these inner needs, and to supply ample opportunity for suitable activity on the part of the pupil.

In practical work, this simple business of education is beset with untold difficulties, arising from inadequacies of actual condition and development on the part of teacher and taught, as well as from perversions and interferences, due to hosts of unforeseen and uncontrollable influences. There is need for much guarding and correcting, bidding and forbidding, preventing and compelling; yet the aims of all these labors look towards the adjustment of surround-ings or the supply of opportunities for activity.

The processes of psychological development follow, in their essential features, the general laws of organic development, manifested also on the physical side of being. There is here, too, a more or less active apprehension and taking-in of material for growth from without, a separation as in digestion, of the serviceable from the unserviceable, an absorption of the serviceable into the mobile contents of the circulatory system of the memory, an assimilation from this in the various higher forms of the mental organism, and, ultimately, full participation of the assimilated portions in the conscious spontaneity of the mind. There are, too, processes of substitution of new thought-material for old, processes of waste, of wear and tear, of death and decay, processes by which unsuitable, effete, injurious material is expelled, and many similiar analogies that remind us of the unity of law presiding over the diversity of phase even in this most complex of facts, the human being.

These laws of development, however, are laws of organic being, and have no bearing upon the fundamental character of the various phases as such. The psychological cannot become physiological, nor the physical spiritual, though the manifestations of these phases naturally correspond with the development of the being of which they are phases.

Thus physical development means more compact, stronger, more active muscles, and a better adaptation of physical life to material conditions. Mental development means more vigorous, more intense, more vivid mind-power, and a nearer approach to objective truth in subjective convictions; moral development means purer feelings, better regulated appetites, stronger will, firmer character, higher aims in life, a keener sense of responsibility, and a deeper appreciation of the relationship that binds all to all.

Organic development, and, therefore, psychological development requires time, *i. e.*, it is, relatively speaking,
slow; it is gradual, continuous, self-active, — psychological
self-activity implying spontaneity of purpose and freedom
of action.

It seems unnecessary for the purpose of this essay to
carry the analysis any farther. The relative slowness,
gradualness, continuity, and self-activity of psychological
development, its primary conditions, and its course, furnish
satisfactory criteria for methods, courses of study, appliances,
and other matters that enter into the details of the work of
teaching.

The proximate end of teaching is the communication of
knowledge. Training, or the systematic guidance of conduct, is not teaching, but may be used for purposes of
teaching, as also teaching may be taken into the service of
training. Together they comprise the chief activities of
the educator in his direct intercourse with the pupil. Their
ultimate end is the same, and lies in education; but teaching approaches it on the side of knowledge, and is primarily
concerned with impressions, while training approaches it
on the side of conduct, and is primarily concerned with
actions. Without training, knowledge is barren; without
teaching, conduct is blind. Teaching gives freedom to
conduct; training gives mastership to knowledge. Teaching leads in, training leads out.

In discussing the application of psychological principles
to the work of teaching, it will, then, be necessary to consider training and leading-out processes in so far as they influence by reaction the leading-in processes, the accumula-
tion of knowledge, both in character and extent.

Another limitation of the subject is found in the fact that

the teaching here contemplated is not teaching in its widest
sense, but comprises in the life of the pupil only that portion of teaching which comes within the control of professional teachers.

In its widest sense, teaching is almost co-extensive with
education, which in the natural life of man stretches from
the cradle to the grave.   Shortly after the birth of the
child and for a period of several years, the parents and
other home-folks busy themselves in purposely increasing
the child's knowledge and liberating its conduct.   At the
age of five, six, or seven the child enters school, where it
passes a few hours during certain days of the week, chiefly
for purposes of instruction.   Yet, even during this period,
which rarely extends beyond the eighteenth year of age,
the school does not control all the teaching.   The home
continues its work; and certain groups of persons (companions, churches, associations) become interested in the
child, and add their teaching efforts, helping or hindering
the work of the school according to the character of their
purposes.   After this period, the child, or young human
being, is left mainly to himself to choose more or less consciously and freely, among the numberless sources of
knowledge, those that may aid him more or less effectually
in earnest efforts of self-education, or that gratify a more
or less egotistical pursuit of pleasure.

The consideration of other limitations that may present
themselves in the individuality of child or teacher, in
heredity, in surroundings, and other equally variable or un-
stable factors in life, must be left to a more detailed discussion than the limits of this essay will admit.

These limitations, however, do not affect the value of
the psychological principles indicated in the first part of
this essay as criteria of the work of professional teaching

in all its phases. In matter and method, in the presentation and arrangement of subjects, it should constantly consider the relative slowness, the gradualness and continuity of psychological development; it should respect and stimulate self-activity; it should regard primary conditions, controlling the character of surroundings with reference to inner needs and supplying at every step ample opportunity for suitable activity. It should keep in view the course of psychological development, the fact that all higher forms of knowledge rest upon the lower; that perception presupposes sensations, and that these imply impressions; that conception feeds upon perceptions, and that reason is built upon the intellect; that impressions can reach insight only through all the intermediate phases, and that whatever blossoms in reason or bears fruit in the will, has its roots far down in the teeming soil of sense-perception. It should keep in view the fact that all that enters consciousness is there irretrievably, that it must travel upward, carrying with it the strength or weakness, the light or darkness of which it is born. It should keep in view the fact that all forms of knowledge are indissolubly bound to corresponding forms of feeling — feelings of attraction or repulsion, of pleasure or pain, which determine in a great measure to what extent the corresponding thought-forms shall participate in the conscious spontaneity of the mind. Lastly, it should keep in view the indispensable need of action for healthy and vigorous thought-growth. It is through action that knowledge becomes aware of its power and value, that it learns to love and appreciate itself, that it learns to know itself, as it were. Action furnishes the rounds of the ladder by which knowledge under the mighty incentives of feeling climbs to ever greater heights, out of darkness into light. It is action that makes the knowledge

of one the knowledge of all, that makes progress a distin-
guishing attribute of the race, raising generation after generation upon the shoulders of its predecessors, sounding the
cheering cry of *excelsior!* even for mankind, and making
it through countless ages as one man in the conquest of the
Infinite.

It is not difficult to distinguish in the psychological
development of the individual human being successive
periods during which the successive phases of thought and
feeling manifest a decided predominance in the order of
their development. There is in earliest infancy a *period*
of *sensation*, during which consciousness has not yet learned
to look outward for factors in its dawn of feeling and knowing, a period characterized by a peculiar dreamy inward-
looking expression of the eyes, and by an equally characteristic vagueness and indirectness of the weak muscular
movements attending the sensations.

This is soon followed, still in infancy but extending far
into childhood, by a *period* of *perception*, when the mind
turns outward, begins to recognize its central position, its
sovereign power, — a period characterized by extraordinary
activity inward and outward. The first clear perception
bursts upon the mind like a sun after the short dawn of
the previous period, kindling life in all directions. Whither-
soever the mind turns, it sees the life without; and its desires, growing steadily in number and urgency, keep the
little hands and arms and feet constantly on the move in
efforts to bring this outer life into subjection.

For education as a whole, this is the most important
period of life on account of its fundamental character, and
on account of its persistence. During this period, which
extends its sway far into the growth of intellect, the mind

gathers its materials from which its proudest conceptions, its intensest thoughts and feelings are derived ; during this period, it sets the rounds of the ladder that is to lead up to whatever height it may climb.

The responsibility of adjusting the child's surroundings, of providing opportunities and material for its activity, of guarding, guiding and helping the child during this period, rests chiefly on the parents and the kindergartner. The materials and methods of the kindergarten, as proposed by Froebel, are well adapted to the individual and social wants of the child at this period. The material is so arranged that with its help the child, even with very limited skill and power of control, can reproduce in outward form the essentials of its ideas of things, and thus, through repeated reflected perceptions of its own thoughts, more surely arrive at clear genuine conceptions. The method is such that the child's spontaneity is always helped, and held without compulsion in the direction of the Beautiful, the True, and the Good. Without appreciable friction, the nascent selfishness is deflected into a deep concern in a common welfare, the love of power steers clear of the shoals of despotism towards an open sea of rational freedom, all traces of vandalism vanish before the pleasures of a healthy exercise of constructiveness, the instinct of play is taught to serve distinct purposes and to become a spirit of work.

The kindergarten, if conducted in accordance with Froebel's suggestions, liberates the intellect, and thus hastens the transition of the child to the third period of psychological development, *the period of conception,* without danger to the solidity, compactness, and harmony of mental growth. During this period, with which this essay is more particularly concerned, the mind turns towards itself as an object.

It compares its notions of things with the things themselves, thus steadily correcting the former, rendering them
by slow degrees more and more accurate, more and more
"true." It compares its notions of things with each other,
and, in accordance with certain differences and resem-
blances, arranges them in groups and classes to which all
its subsequent mental gain is referred. In due time proximate groups are united on the basis of deeper similarities
in remoter groups; and this process is continued on successively higher planes, until the mind learns to hold all
in a few simple terms, such as space and time.

A deep and abiding interest rivets the mind to these
activities. In its efforts to bring ideas nearer to objective
truth, it patiently *observes* the external through long periods
of time, continually strengthening or modifying previous
notions in the light of new perceptions, with an honesty
and conscientiousness that partake of highest virtue ; for
the purpose of determining the true sequence of cause and
effect, it subjects the external in painstaking and laborious
experiment to certain conditions, again and again.

Through such processes it gradually arrives in various
directions at systematically connected criteria of knowledge, which it dignifies with the name of *Science*, whose
mastery demands the closest application and not unfrequently kindles an interest capable of filling a life.

The fields of science furnish the soil that yields to genius,
in all its forms and powers, however humble or exalted,
the harvest of inventions and discoveries, of creations and
revelations that lift him upward and teach him his origin
and his destiny.

The greater portion of this period falls within the limits
of the school, which is the chief concern of this essay.
During this period, the mind rises consciously from the

concrete to the abstract, from the particular to the general, from the actual to the possible, from the outer to the inner, from experience to principle, from facts to laws, from complexity to simplicity, from the extensive to the intensive, from space to time ; and the business of the teacher is to adjust surroundings, and to guide and guard the pupil with reference to these activities, so that in the period of insight, reason may not fail him, and the will may become duly liberated.

I propose to show by way of illustration, the application of the psychological principles heretofore enunciated in the following typical phases of the work of teaching: 1. A general outline of a "course of study" within the limits of Primary and Grammar Schools ; 2. school organization, with reference to the distribution of teachers and pupils; 3. method of elementary reading and writing ; 4, spirit of disciplinary regulations.

In framing a course of study for Primary and Grammar Schools it should be constantly borne in mind that the period involved corresponds chiefly to the earlier portion of the psychological period of conception. When the child enters school it is still gathering perceptions, though upon some things it has quite clear and comprehensive conceptions ; and when it leaves the grammar school, its intellect should have grown into a fair supremacy, and the dawn of insight into the deeper relations of being should be full upon its mind. During the first years of school-life, the subjects of study should be of a character to facilitate the formation of perceptions and their transition into comprehensive conceptions; they should lie on the side of the concrete, the actual, the outer ; they should deal with experiences, with facts, with space, with objects. They should, then, gradually merge into forms that lie on the side of the abstract, the possible, the inner; that deal with principles, with laws, with time, steadily leading the child out of the complexity of things into the simplicity of thought.

Now, the school can afford neither the time nor the labor that would be required to follow the child,— explaining, guiding, and warning — through the maze of facts and phenomena as they occur in nature, and the confusion of practical experiences of an undisciplined life. It must invent more or less artificial surroundings, a world of objects and events more or less idealized, more or less systematized, where the child may attain a fair understanding of the essentials of life with as little friction as possible. This ideal world must be the child's and within the child's control. The child must not, as in object-lessons, be placed at respectful distances from certain sample-pieces thereof, and taught to repeat certain phrases concerning these; but it must have objects and material placed within its hands to be fully its own for purposes of observation, experiment, analysis, or construction. Again, these objects placed within the child's reach, and with the help of which it is to attain the intellectual control of a world, should present their essential characteristics in unmistakable distinctness, in striking and unavoidable contrasts; and they should be such that the child can handle them not only without injury to itself and these objects, but with profit to both.

Abundant hints in this direction have been given by Froebel in the construction of his gifts, each of which represents in a form readily controlled some simple essential fact or relation, whose full apprehension throws a new flood of light upon the child's world. Playing with the simple blocks, tablets, sticks, lentil seeds or dots, and working with sheets of paper, paper strips, the weaving-sheet, pasteboard, the embroidery-needle, the drawing-slate, sand or clay, the child obtains successively clear notions and full control of various laws of position and shape, divisibility and number, size and gravitation, symmetry and proportionality of parts, and other relations and qualities which constitute the essentials of things.

With the help of this simple material, the child is enabled to form concrete representations of the essentials of things, in form, number, relations of position, etc., immeasurably nearer the conceptions of the things involved than are the things themselves; thus the formation of clear conceptions and, consequently, the liberation of language and of the intellect, are hastened without detriment to the solidity and compactness of mental growth.

The essentials of the outer world that interest man most nearly in his efforts to obtain intellectual control of his surroundings are centered in *space*, which in its limits involves *form, position, size, direction,* and *number*. Of these, number and size have a special interest, inasmuch as they constitute the chief bridges in the transition of the mind from outer space to inner time. To these may be added *color* as an important element, depending on certain relations of material surfaces to light. Lying nearer the emotional side of sensation, it has much power to arouse interest in related elements of space, hence its educational value is very great. The school will, then, find the first subjects for instruction with reference to the pupil's individual development, in the provinces of *Geometry, Drawing, Coloring,* and *Arithmetic*.

Almost simultaneously, however, the phenomena of motion and life to which the changes of position, direction,

size, form and number among surrounding objects are
referred, and which intensely affect the child's comfort and
welfare, point to studies connected with the provinces of
Physics, Chemistry, Natural History, Geography, and
Uranography.

Long before the child's entrance in school, too, the helpful presence of others aroused in its heart feelings of gratitude, of affection, and good will. These may or may not
have been brought more clearly to the child's consciousness,
and more fully within its control in the social games and
group-work of the kindergarten. Howsoever this may be,
the school should afford constant opportunity for social
enterprises, involving common interests, common purposes,
and common efforts, leading to an interest in the occupations of men, and the relationships among men. This leads
to studies connected with *Sociology* and *History,* through
which man connects himself consciously with the Past.

In all that relates to motion and life and, consequently, to
the social phases of being, *sound* — lying also nearer the
emotional side of sensation — plays a part similar to that
of color in the realms of space. Connected with rhythm
in the harmonious combinations and melodious successions
of *music,* — it has wonderful power in freeing the mind
from the material, and leading it to the spiritual, and is,
therefore, of incalculable value in lifting man to the highest
planes of mental life.

The chief medium of the work of teaching is *language.*
At the moment when the child is awakened to self-consciousness, language appears as the chief outward reaction
of growing self-consciousness in the intercourse with
others. Language binds man to man, makes the Past an
ingredient of the Present, and holds this fast for a Future.
In the development of the intellect and of reason, it is

the medium of thought, the indispensable condition of their growth. Hence language, with all that pertains to it, will furnish subjects of instruction during the entire school-life.

Among the many considerations of method which it would be necessary to discuss in an exhaustive treatise on the subject involved, before deciding upon a "course of study," I refer here only to two of the most important.

The first of these is the necessity of a concentric arrangement of the subjects of study. This demands that, at each successive stage, the subject come to the child as a whole, that all the roots of the knowledge and skill involved be represented within the limits of the child's capacity. This, *the child's capacity*, and not the possibilities of the subject, furnishes the criteria for decision. From itself as a center, the mind penetrates in successive efforts, in circles or spheres constantly widening in all directions to ever greater depths of insight, to ever greater powers of control.

Another equally important consideration is the constant need of opportunities for adequate, all-sided expression on the part of the pupil both in language and in manual activity. This keeps alive the mightiest incentive for advancement, the sensation of power, and prepares the pupil for the business of life, which means expression in some form, of what is in him.

For the sake of showing the practical bearings of these considerations in unmistakable distinctness, I present below, without further comment, from a course framed in accordance with these requirements, the outline of a first circle or sphere. It comprises the first two years of school-life in a system of graded schools, the child entering at the average age of six years.

FIRST CIRCLE. (Two years.)
FIRST GROUP OF SUBJECTS: *Form, Drawing, Coloring.*

1. *Form:* Recognition and naming of the cube, cylinder, sphere, pyramid, and cone; of the square, lozenge, triangle, hexagon, octagon, pentagon, the circle, semicircle, quadrant, and oval; diagonal, diameter, radius, center; straight, curved, wavy, and spiral lines; of parallel, diverging, oblique, and perpendicular, horizontal, vertical, and slanting directions; right, obtuse, and acute angles. — Materials used; clay for modeling, tablets, splints, papers for folding and cutting, paper-strips, etc.

2. *Drawing:* Automatic exercises by dictation or otherwise, in simple, symmetrical arrangements, in networks, embodying squares, half-squares, equilateral-triangles, with circumscribed and inscribed circles, or arcs; language-drawing or conception-drawing (p. 25), in simple outline representations of things, involving only essentials; artistic drawing in symmetrical combinations involving squares and circles with their subdivisions, shading and hatching, leaves, flowers, fruits, birds, and butterflies. The slate, properly prepared paper, the folding-sheet, the sand-table, and clay-tablet yield suitable drawing surfaces. The use of the dividers is admissible, especially with the clay-tablet and the folding-sheet.

3. *Coloring:* Classifying beads, dots, colored worsteds by their colors; "rainbow-games" with these and the paint-brush or colored crayon; coloring squares, triangles, circles, etc., in symmetrical arrangements on white folding-sheet, ruled paper, or clay-tablet; coloring leaves, flowers, fruits, birds, and butterflies.

SECOND GROUP OF SUBJECTS: *Number* and *Size.*

1. *Number:* Counting "forward and backward" by one's, two's, three's, four's, and five's, addition, subtraction, mul-

tiplication, measuring, and division within the limits (in successive sub-circles), of 1 to 10, 1 to 20, 1 to 100, 1 to 1000; similar operations, at the same time, with fractions within the limits, in corresponding sub-circles, of halves to fifths, halves to tenths, halves to twentieths (excluding 11ths, 13ths, 17ths, 19ths), and halves to hundredths (excluding all difficult denominations) ; games of exchange, of buying and selling, involving at first only price, but subsequently also gain and loss; games of "giving" and "guessing." Material used: tablets, splints, paper-strips, beans, buttons, etc.

2. *Size.* (Measurements): measuring and estimating length, distances, areas in inches, feet, yards; liquid and dry measures of capacity; lifting and weighing, within reasonable limits; games of manufacturing and jobbing.

THIRD GROUP OF SUBJECTS : *Physical and Chemical Properties, Natural History, Geography and Uranography.*

1. *Physical and Chemical Properties :* Classifying substances by their weight, hardness, smoothness of surface, solubility, fusibility, combustibility, and similar properties. Suitable collections of substances may be placed in the children's hands, or made by them.

2. *Natural History :* Observation of plant-growth, classifying of leaves, flowers, fruits, roots, plants, and animals by certain prominent characteristics. Collection and description of plants; observation and description of animals.

3. *Geography and Uranography :* Names of days, months and seasons, observation of Sun's position at stated times, course of sun in different seasons ; changes of moon ; cardinal points of compass ; counting rainy days and days of sunshine; localities of plants and animals ; stories of remarkable plants and animals living in distant countries ; sketches of school-room, the school, the home, the way to

school, certain prominent localities; bird's-eye views on sand-table.

FOURTH GROUP OF SUBJECTS: *Sociology and History.*

1. *Sociology:* Social games, dramatizations of the occupations of men; construction of railroads, canals, bridges, tunnels, etc., on the sand-tables; discussion and dramatization of home and school-relations.

2. *History:* Accounts of events in the child's life; anecdotes from the lives of children.

FIFTH GROUP OF SUBJECTS: *Language and Music.*

1. *Language:* Conversation (not catechizing) is at the very soul of all the exercises heretofore mentioned. In addition, there are special exercises in the reading and writing of simple sentences and words; in word-building from sound-elements found with or by the children; in contrasting and combining classes of words in accordance with a variety of criteria of form, sound, meaning, or construction; in labeling and taking notes in connection with other subjects of study; in the writing of short orders, accounts, letters and stories; in reading for pleasure or profit from books and periodicals within the scope of the child's powers.

2. *Music:* appears incidentally in the social games and dramatizations of the Fourth Group; but there should be special exercises in which the child is drilled in the recognition and production of sounds in pitch, relative duration, in melodious and harmonious arrangement. The inherent emotional qualities of music are brought to the child's consciousness with the help of marches led by thoughtful improvisations on a musical instrument.

A course similar to this, satisfies the child's intellectual wants in all directions; it is well rounded, as a whole and in all its parts; it never leaves the child's knowledge in a fragmentary condition. The child can and does constantly make use of all it learns for the immediate purposes of its life, and its school is indeed a preparation for life. Every new circle does not so much complete the knowledge previously gained ; but, starting again from the same center, the child, it extends this knowledge to wider fields and greater depths; and all the time, the development of tact and skill, of taste and foresight in the application keeps pace with the new acquisitions. Thus, in due time, science may be reached on the side of knowledge, and art on the side of skill.

In considering the distribution of teachers and pupils, it is to be taken for granted that the teachers are well fitted for their work in professional knowledge and skill, as well as in all the qualities of head and heart, needed for the work. The question then rests wholly with the individual and social wants of the child, and these point unmistakably to the desirability of grading. These wants will be best satisfied among those who belong to the same circle of development. Here the child will find the material best adapted to its requirements ; in these surroundings it will feel the keenest interest, and find the readiest appreciation. Where it is feasible, even the children of sub-circles should be arranged in separate groups. By the union of contiguous circles the attention of the pupil and the energies of the teacher become scattered, and there is great loss of interest on the one hand, and of power and efficiency, on the other. This is quite apparent in some country district schools, where children of all grades are united. If these schools ever attain an alleged superiority, it is due chiefly to the fact that they do not hinder development, whereas badly conducted graded schools, built on fragmentary

courses of study, do positive harm by repressing, deflect-
ing, or unsettling development in a variety of ways.

On the other hand, it is desirable that occasions be provided at more or less regular intervals, when the children
of contiguous circles are brought together for exercises
more or less festive in character. Here the younger are
encouraged by the joy and help they can give to the older
whom they esteem so highly; and the higher achievements
of the latter of which they are witnesses, furnish whole-
some and fertilizing incentives to effort, while the older
pupils are taught to feel the joy of leadership and the responsibility of example.

In the transfers from one circle to another, the degree
and character of mental development should furnish the
chief criteria, the amount of knowledge and skill acquired
being indeed significant, but of secondary importance. The
practice of deciding wholly by the amount of positive knowledge acquired, is pernicious. A certain degree of intellectual maturity will be sure to reach in the various subjects of
study a bearable equality with agreeable and helpful companions, under the leadership of a tactful teacher. On the
other hand, a pupil whose advanced intellectual powers are
condemned by lack of knowledge in certain directions or
details to confine themselves to inadequate material and
within a forcibly contracted scope, will lose interest and
waste life, and will exercise by contagion a baneful influence even upon otherwise well-conditioned companions.

The teacher should follow her pupils at least through
the phases of one circle and, if possible, through more
circles than one. This avoids the friction of becoming
acquainted with each other, and the consequent loss of
energy and interest. Indeed, this is necessary in order
to secure on the part of the teacher that interest in the

child as such, and on the part of the pupil that faith in the good will of the teacher, which are so essential to success.

In settling upon suitable methods of teaching the arts of reading and writing, it should be kept in mind that reading and writing do not constitute language, but only those phases thereof, respectively, in which expressions in language are fixed in symbols for an indefinite period, or in which expressions so fixed are deciphered for purposes of pleasure and profit. Reading and writing should at all times be so managed that the child may make full use of all it learns for the purposes of its life in and out of school. The matter should be kept within the scope of the child's powers of understanding and appreciation, and should be presented in a shape that will provoke the child's self-active efforts in the use and practice of these arts.

Here, as elsewhere, the necessary simple cognitions should be obtained from a concrete outer complexity, by processes of analysis; and all elements thus gained should be successively verified and fixed by varied use in all-sided synthesis. Strictly, therefore, the teacher should begin with suitable sentences, from which the child obtains by analysis certain words, which may be used in new combinations for a variety of purposes. From these words it descends by new analysis to more or less complex combinations of sounds and, ultimately to simple sounds, and uses these again in word-building. However, it is perfectly safe, in most cases, to begin at once with the analysis of words, inasmuch as the child usually reaches the word-stage before entering school, even if it has not had the benefit of the kindergarten.

The words for the first teaching should be selected from the child's experience and conversational vocabulary, so that they may be to the child genuine symbols of ideas of actual things, and not mere arbitrary combinations of sounds. These words should be simple, too, in form and sound, easily recognized and readily used in plain state-ments by the child, conditions that are fulfilled by mono-syllables that embody short vowel-sounds. The child may be interested in a number of these by short stories, con-versations and pictures, e. g., — *dog, rat, trap, cat, fish, net, pot, pin,* etc; *wet, fat, black, hot, thin,* etc; *can, run, swim, purr,* etc. To these should be added in the first or second exercise, a few such words as, — *the, is, in, my;* and the child is ready for sentence-building to a limited extent. It may form sentences such as, — the dog can run, the cat is fat, the rat can run, the rat is in the trap, the fish is in the net, the pot is hot, my dog is thin, etc., in a variety of speaking and writing games in which the teacher gives some portion of a statement which the pupil completes, and *vice versa.*

Experience shows that the child has little difficulty and is much interested in writing these words and sentences in legible script from the very outset. On the other hand, the practice of printing involves a serious loss of time, in-asmuch as it teaches something which under ordinary cir-cumstances, the child must unlearn again. For similar reasons capital letters should be correctly used from the very beginning.

In a short time, the words thus used become in their turn objects of interest and thought, and, consequently, of analysis. This may be hastened by exercises in which words of similar sound are arranged in sets, orally and in writing, e. g. :

dog	cat	fish	net	pot	can	
hog	hat	dish	wet	hot	man	etc
log	fat	wish	pet	dot	pan	

From such sets, by proper treatment, the child will obtain, more or less complex sound-elements, like *og, at, ish, et, ot*, etc.; and simple consonant elements like *d, l, h*, etc. These consonant elements may be kept before the child, on some convenient part of the blackboard, in suitable arrangement, — b, c (k), d, f, g, h, etc. The child will, then, enjoy games in word-building, by uniting the complex sound-elements with the consonant elements and making "words that have a meaning." Thus *og* will yield *bog, dog, fog, hog, log; at* will furnish *bat, cat, fat, hat, mat, pat, rat, sat, vat, that, chat; an* will lead to *can, fan, man, pan, ran, tan, van, than*, etc. In all cases the child should prove its findings by embodying the words in suitable sentences, in exercises involving both speaking and writing.

By subsequent analytical processes the complex elements yield their simpler constituents: *og, at, ish, an*, etc., reveal themselves respectively as *o – g, a – t, i – sh, a – n*, etc.; and these furnish the material with which the child, at the hand of properly arranged synthetical processes, may rise to whatever complexity the language affords.

It might be shown now how the regular long vowel-sounds are discovered, and how so-called irregular spellings may be fixed in contrast games, involving sets of words like the following :

mat – mate	male – mail
hat – hate	sale – sail
man – mane	tale – tail
can – cane	see – sea
pan – pane	feet – feat
fin – fine	meet – meat
pin – pine	reed – read
etc.	etc.

It might be further shown, how in a different direction, words may be contrasted or grouped according to their meanings or their places in speech, involving a multitude of exercises similar to the following:

1. good – bad high – low light – dark straight – curved	2. up – down in – out above – below before – behind
3. good – goodness great – greatness dark – darkness quick – quickness	4. slow – slowly great – greatly quiet – quietly sweet – sweetly
5. snow – white coal – black fire – hot	6. dog – barks cat – mews horse – runs
7. bake – baker read – reader write – writer	8. tastes { sweet / sour runs { fast / slow looks { young / old
9. animal faithful } dog barks	10. fruit yellow } lemon sour

It will be seen that these suggestions, collectively and separately, satisfy in every particular the requirements indicated on page 23. There is throughout the upward tendency from the concrete to the abstract, from particulars to the general, from the actual to the possible, from the outer to the inner, from experience to principle, from facts to law, from the complexity of things to the simplicity of thought. They deal throughout with material which the child is supposed to control fully; and all it learns it can at once apply to the purposes of its life, in arranging and sifting whatever knowledge it has, as well as in communication with others in written and spoken language.

Among the many exercises that may be invented in this direction, I call attention to the use which the child may make of its skill in reading and writing, in labeling the collections it may be induced to make, collections of leaves, of metals, of stones, of kinds of wood, of flower-names, of names of animals, of simple conception-drawings, of observations on the weather, etc., as indicated on page 29, etc. The details of all this, however, and of other applications not mentioned here, must be left to the tact of the teacher who has entered fully into the spirit of psychological laws, and who has the courage to let the children grow.

As soon as the child has acquired a tolerable control of the principal sounds and letters in script, certainly as soon as it has accomplished the work indicated on page 35, the child may be introduced to the printed letters. These are sufficiently like the script letters to recall them in the child's mind almost at first sight, more especially if they appear on suitable printed cards in combinations or words with which the child is familiar. Loose sheets, small hand charts, little books, containing very short stories, incidents, anecdotes, riddles, concise descriptive statements concerning plants, animals, and other objects of interest, and as soon as possible, suitable " storybooks," books of travel, and books of reference should be provided, so that the child may learn to turn to the printed page, from the very start, for legitimate purposes of pleasure and instruction

Henceforth, there should be a steady advance in all

directions. In gradual, continuous progress the pupil should
be led, though always in accordance with the principles
enounced at the outset, to a genuine, self-active appreciation of the science and art garnered in the printed page.
There should be exercises in which the pupil acquires
interest and skill in culling knowledge from books, and
others in which he may kindle his own enthusiasm for the
Beautiful, the True, and the Good, at the immortal fires
that burn in treasures of literature ; exercises in which he
records concisely and systematically the results of his own
observation and experience, and others in which he learns
to reproduce in beautiful, living speech, for the enjoyment
and edification of others, the words that glowed in the
innermost heart of a Past, as well as the emotions that
tremble in his own breast.

In the selection of material for these purposes it should
be remembered, however, that these exercises, like all
others in which the pupil engages, should take the key-
note, not from the possibilities of the subject, but from the
actualities and possibilities of the pupil's mental development at the respective stage. To force or induce a pupil
to memorize formulas of knowledge beyond his ken, or to
reproduce in outer semblance, emotions he cannot appreciate, breeds hopeless self-conceit and hypocrisy, blunts and
vitiates, or, even, destroys in his spirit all that is meant to
raise him to his destiny. On the other hand, if the material is presented to the pupil, at successive stages, in forms
at which he can aim with reasonable hope of success, in
the exercise of his productive activity, he will in due time
attain an all-sided mastery of the arts involved, commensu-
rate with his powers, and adequate to the purposes and
aims of his life.

The question of disciplinary regulations runs through every phase of school-work, and is, consequently, of the greatest importance. Discipline is concerned more or less directly with the morals of the pupil. It begins when the child begins to become more or less consciously a part of some social organism, and its general aim is the intro-ordination of the child into these organisms. It would make the child an integral part of the organisms in question, without impairing his individual interest and his personal liberty; or, rather, it would direct the development of the child's individual interests and personal aspirations, in harmony with the welfare of the social organism.

In the family, the common interests center largely in the growing individuality of the child, in whom the family sees the promise of its perpetuation. Here the child is introduced, as it were, to itself; here it discovers and exercises its powers with almost exclusive reference to the pleasures of activity. During the first years of the child's life, at least, the disciplinary activity of the family is chiefly yielding, provident, protecting, mostly confined to the adjustment of surroundings with reference to the child's needs and wants. This remains as the prevailing characteristic of the ideal family throughout the child's life, and the adult child returns to the bosom of his father's house with a sense of trust and security which he can find in no other place, not even in the house founded by himself.

In the kindergarten, the child is introduced to its equals; and, while the development of individual powers still receives a very large share of attention, the surroundings are so adjusted that the child meets in the exercise of its individual powers, at every step, the need of help from its play-follows and the opportunity of giving help to them. The activities and aspirations, suggested by the surround-

ings, constantly point to the value of common effort, of co-
operation.   The successes and pleasures this society brings,
are so much greater and more intense than those to which
it can aspire single-handed, that there is born in the child's
heart a sense of gratitude which is none the less real because it is selfish, a love which is none the less intense
because it springs from self-love.   In due time the child
overlooks the pleasurable reactions of giving pleasure and
of helping, and begins to find a genuine delight in helpful-
ness and sympathy for their own sake; and love whose
roots are far down in the dark soil of selfishness, begins to
put out beneficent leaves and blossoms in the bright atmos-
phere of a generous good-will.

In the school, the chief aim of disciplinary regulations is
to raise this generous good-will into an abiding sense of
duty or obligation, and to bring the conduct under the conscious control of this sense.   Here the child should learn
to submit cheerfully to unwelcome restraints and to engage
with alacrity in laborious pursuits for the sake of needed
results.   In a measure the family and, more particularly,
the kindergarten have prepared the child for this important
discipline, in leading the child from *play* for immediate
gratification to *work* for the attainment of remote ends,
very much simplifying the work of the school, wherever
such ideal relations exist.   Practically, however, very few
children pass through the kindergarten, and the school is
compelled to do, as well as it can, much of the work properly belonging to an earlier period, or to labor under the
many trying disadvantages that result from a neglect to
establish a solid foundation of good-will.

. The proximate end of discipline is automatic good conduct,—good habits; its proudest outcome is a well-regulated
will.   It appeals, particularly during the earlier periods of

the child's life, much to the emotional side of mental life. During the first period, it wins through pleasurable sensations, by means of which it leads and holds the child's attention to whatever it deems proper. To these it adds, at a later period, the skillful creation of desires, which by equally skillful gratification, it raises to forms akin to an intelligent interest. The school seeks to render this interest abiding and conscious, by a prudent use of pleasurable sensations and of the creation and gratification of desires in connection with the special forms of thought and action with which it is concerned, appealing, however, more and more to the intellect and the reason, through which alone the will can be reached. (p. 13.)

Generally speaking, the discipline of a school will be good in proportion to the interest it may have called forth on the part of the pupil, in its work. Without such interest success is impossible. Stagnation, retrogression, disintegration will surely follow its abatement or loss. On the other hand, this interest will render it a comparatively easy matter to secure the neatness, accuracy, persistence, consciousness, regard for fellow-students, and teachers, respect for the school, and obedience to its minor regulations that are so necessary to the success of the school. Indeed, sweetness of temper, firmness of character, learning, skill, enthusiasm, and other qualities of the teacher owe their value chiefly to their power in eliciting, satisfying, and holding interest.

Whatever brings joy to the child's heart, a pleasing sensation, the gratification of a harmless desire, the innocent exercise of the sense of power; whatever makes life brighter and fuller, whatever makes existence worth more to the child, will be sure to call forth this interest. Whatever the child can use for the purposes of its life, will call forth this interest.

It is, then, in this respect, the business of the school to adjust surroundings so that the child may have ample opportunities to form and attain worthy purposes, so that all it sees and does may strengthen these purposes and raise them to higher planes, liberating the child more and more from the need of guidance, and making it more and more the conscious architect of its own fortune.

The details of this work should be arranged and managed with constant reference to the criteria, indicated on pp. 18–20.

However, the ideal conditions that would render possible a school-discipline, based wholly on interest in the work of the school and on a well-regulated activity of the pupils, are, perhaps, unattainable in practice. The imperfections of the teacher and of the school, the shortcomings of the home and of the kindergarten, the evil effects of uncontrolled associations, and, not unfrequently, of heredity, give rise to a host of unforeseen and unavoidable evils which call for more or less artificial treatment, for the introduction of motives foreign to the work of the school, and for more or less direct compulsion through fear of punishment, dread of authority, or hope of reward.

If these compulsory means of discipline are used humbly, for what they are worth, with the constant prayer for the removal of the shortcomings that render them unavoidable, they will frequently accomplish much good, but in the hands of pride or self-conceit they do incalculable harm.

The most pernicious of these is censure mingled with words of contempt or derision. In the first place, the child deserves, even at the worst, compassion and helpful advice, rather than scorn; and then, these words sink deep into the hearts of the children with meanings they were not intended to have, embittering and warping the disposition more permanently than even unjust chastisement with the rod.

Even gentler forms of censure have their dangers, inasmuch as they involve an arraignment of motives. The child so often does wrong through ignorance or lack of judgment, with the best of motives, and it needs in these cases instruction and advice, but not blame.

However, under all circumstances, practical as well as ideal, the strongest allies of good discipline are good habits, and these can be secured only at the expense of constant watchfulness. The child must be carefully guarded against opportunities or temptations to do wrong, for every such opportunity or temptation retards the formation of a good habit, or weakens a good habit already formed. During a long period, the child does indifferently right or wrong, merely intent on doing something ; but what it does plants a tendency in its mind, which requires only a few similar opportunities to become an eager desire, and, ultimately, to settle into a fixed habit. All that might give rise to such tendencies should be carefully excluded from the child's presence, while opportunities for harmless or beneficent all-sided activity should be plentifully supplied. Thus, in due time, good habits may ripen into firmness of character which is proof against temptation from inherent vigor for good.

www.ingramcontent.com/pod-product-compliance
Lightning Source LLC
Chambersburg PA
CBHW021429090426
42739CB00009B/1422

*9 7 8 3 3 3 7 1 6 5 7 3 4 *